# Endorsement:

The story of Harry and Eddie and their w
is one of the lesser-known stories from World \
in the more dramatic reports of troop movements and bombing raids.
But those who know history realize that the big events sometimes occur
because a few little people showed up and did the right thing at the
right time – in the midst of confusing situations. Dr. Beverly Boulware
tells this charming story from a point of view that encourages readers,
both old and young, to value friendships built on shared suffering and
shared efforts; where trust was developed and deepened long before the
day when the trusted friend showed up on the stage of history at just
the right moment.

*-JoAnn G. Magnuson*
*Holocaust Educator and Curator Jewish-Christian Library Center, Minneapolis, Minnesota*

*Harry and Eddie: The Friendship that Changed the World* is a factual, little
known story of a strong friendship that resulted in US support for the
creation of Israel, a new country where homeless Jewish people could
live after the ruins of World War II.  It is a story of mutual trust, hard
work, and strong character.  This account of Harry Truman and Eddie
Jacobson begins with a description of their families, which reflects their
brotherly bond, and follows them through their lives.  Boulware shares
details not found in textbooks that allow readers to understand the real
life struggles of these influential men and their places in history.  The
strong structure and sequencing of events show how two very different
men were also very much alike.

*-Mary Kay Moskal, Ed.D.*
*Associate Dean, Kalmanovitz School of Education*
*Saint Mary's College of California*

What an informative and inspiring book! Through the true story of
a lifetime friendship between two common-yet-great men, the author
reveals little-known details about the formation of the State of Israel.
Further, the story is engaging and accessible to a wide range of readers.
Even more so, the content challenges people of faith to think deeply
about how God works in His own time, in His own ways, to bring

to pass His will. In the case of Harry Truman and Eddie Jacobson, we can clearly see that He bridged theological divides among responsive individuals to fulfill His divine purpose for people and for nations. Perhaps within this story we will renew our trust that, even in our seemingly mindless and heartless chaotic world, God is truly in control and can use all things for our good and His glory. Perhaps, too, we will renew our commitment to sharing the eternal Peace accessible only through Him.

*-Dr. Eula Ewing Monroe*
*Professor of Mathematics Education, Brigham Young University*

There are many good lessons for everyone to learn and use from this story which makes this book very valuable. The lessons flow from the situations in the story into the life of the reader. It is worth being in your library. For sure, it is worth reading and passing along to family and friends and everyone who is interested in the return of the people back to their homeland.

*-Mrs. Roberta Hromas*
*President, American Christian Trust*

Take one protestant Missourian, destined to become President of the United States and one Jewish businessman from Missouri; mix them together through World Wars and problems resulting from wars. What do we get? An incredible true story between two great gentlemen who forged a friendship during a war, persevered as friends beyond wars, and found common ground amid a myriad of differences to provide solutions for the hundreds of people displaced because of these wars. This is a story of the strength and power of friendship. A wonderful, worthwhile read with historical value for middle school students.

*-Dr. Kathleen Sanders*
*Professor Advanced Education Programs,*
*Coordinator of the MSE/Reading Specialist Program, Fort Hays State University*

Having read this book of the friendship that had changed the world, written by Prof. Beverly Joan Boulware, made me think about so many things that the American young generation can learn from it. No doubt that for me being a child of two Holocaust survivors, a Holocaust researcher who teaches at a University in Israel and a mother of two teenage children– the importance of this book, *"Harry and Eddie"* is very clear. Through this book American youngsters can learn not only about this beautiful friendship between these two important men, but also learn significant information about the tragic chapter in Jewish history: the Holocaust (the systematic murder of the Jewish people in Europe during World War II, by the Nazis and their collaborators). This book also sheds light on the creation of the State of Israel as the historic homeland of the Jewish people, and addresses the role of Harry and Eddie in the establishment of Israel. I hope that this book will encourage more young people to learn about these historical chapters, and by that, will contribute to the development of the friendship between the two nations: The USA and Israel, in the future.

*-Dr. Ronit Fisher*
*University of Haifa, Department of Jewish History*

"Want to know the story behind one of the big miracles that gave birth to the state of Israel? Then pick up *Harry and Eddie: The Friendship that Changed the World!* This seldom told but powerful story of the friendship of two men – one Jewish and the other Christian – shaped the course of human history. Beverly Joan Boulware tells this profound story in a way both youngsters and adults will appreciate. It's a great reminder as Ben Franklin once said, "That God governs in the affairs of men!" As one who has seen the modern day miracle firsthand, I highly recommend it!

*-Chris Mitchell*
*CBN News Middle East Bureau Chief*

"I am aware of the close relationship that President Truman and Eddie Jacobson shared and how Eddie played an important role in the President's decision to support the establishment of the modern state of Israel. Joan's wonderful book brings a much deeper understanding of their relationship and its importance in the President's commitment to support Israel and the Jewish people. I rejoice that this story is being made available to the youth of our generation and beyond."

*The Rev. Sam Clarke*
*Anglican/Episcopal Minister (retired)*
*First Director of Christian Friends of Yad Vashem, the Holocaust Museum and Memorial in Jerusalem, Israel.*

# Harry and Eddie

*The Friendship that Changed the World*

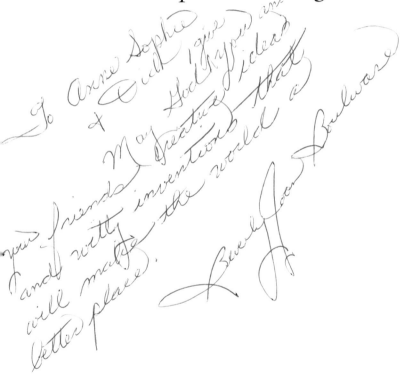

To Anne Sophie
& Dick, I give
you my
Heartfelt ideas
May future ideas
and witty inventions that
will make the world a
better place.

Beverly Joan Boulware

## Beverly Joan Boulware

Harry & Eddie Publishing LLC / Nashville

## Introduction:

Remember, remember, remember people like my dad and Mr. Truman who embraced the challenges in their lives. Both men were presented with opportunities to help others. They used the resources available and applied principles of reason to pursue answers to the problems faced by their generation.

*~ Elinor Jacobson Borenstine (daughter of Eddie Jacobson)*

"The choice for our people, Mr. President, is between statehood and extermination. History and providence have placed this issue in your hands, and I am confident that you will yet decide it in the spirit of the moral law."

~ Taken from Chaim Weizmann's letter to Harry S. Truman, 9 April 1948
Truman Papers, Harry S. Truman Library, Independence, Missouri.

# Dedication

I dedicate this book to Esther Cohen Levens. When Esther first shared with me about Eddie Jacobson's historic meeting with Harry Truman to plead for the Jews, I was moved by the friendship between the two men. As an educator, I wanted to record the story to share with my students the importance of relationships.

Mrs. Levens made possible the contact with Elinor Jacobson Borenstine, daughter of Eddie Jacobson. In addition, as a friend of the Jacobson family, Mrs. Levens was able to add details to the story that few would have ever known.

Esther and her husband, the late Vrem Levens, were among those who worked tirelessly and sacrificed much in the Kansas City area to raise American support for the State of Israel.

**Publisher:** Harry & Eddie Publishing LLC
            1000 Pearl Road
            Pleasantville TN 37033

Harry and Eddie may be purchased at special quantity discounts. Resale opportunities are available for donor programs, fund raising, book clubs, or other educational purposes for schools and universities. For more information contact:
Mel Cohen mel@inspiredauthorspress.com

Have Beverly Joan Boulware speak at your school, university, fundraiser or special event. Contact Joan at joan@harryandeddiebook.com

This publication is designed to provide accurate and authoritative information. It is sold with the understanding that the author or the publisher is not engaged in rendering historical or professional services. Effort has been made to verify accurate Internet addresses. The author and the publisher assume no responsibility for Internet address errors.

**For licensing or bulk sales:** Mel Cohen mel@inspiredauthorspress.com

1. Israel   2. History   3. President Harry S. Truman   4. World War I   5. Friendships
6. Loyalty      7. Decisions   8. The Jewish People   9. World War II   10. Holocaust
I. Beverly Joan Boulware II. Harry and Eddie: The Friendship that Changed the World

ISBN Print: 978-0-9966218-0-9
ISBN eBook: 978-0-9966218-1-6
ISBN ePDF: 978-0-9966218-2-3
Library of Congress Control Number:  2015913960


Author: Beverly Joan Boulware
Edited by Anne Severance, Mel Cohen
Cover and Interior Design by Jared Rowe
Publishing Consultant: Mel Cohen of Inspired Authors Press
www.inspiredauthorspress.com
Website: www.harryandeddiebook.com

## Acknowledgments

I want to thank my publishing consultant, Mel Cohen, for his tremendous contribution to all aspects of the publication process. I would also like to thank Anne Severance, the copy editor and Jared Rowe for his help with the cover and interior design. In addition, I appreciate the input and encouragement of the following people who helped make this book possible: Marianne, Marcy, JoAnn, Roberta, Marilyn, Eula, Pat, Becki, Cheryl, Angela, Judy, Kim, Kathy, Charlen, Jimmi and Jill.

Harry Truman and Eddie Jacobson did not know their friendship would one day change history.

Their backgrounds were so different. Eddie's parents, David and Sarah Jacobson, were of the Orthodox Jewish faith. His grandfather was a refugee from Lithuania who came to America to escape the Russian army. His mother's family was of German descent. After Eddie was born, they moved from New York to Kansas to live near her sister because his mother was struggling with ill health. Eddie and his siblings understood many of the difficulties of immigrants. English was not the first language of their grandparents, and they were very poor. His father was a tailor and worked hard to support his wife and six children.

Harry, a Missourian by birth, the son of John and Martha Young Truman, was born and reared in Western Missouri near Kansas City. His family was Protestant, from the Baptist and Presbyterian denominations. His parents, grandparents and even great-grandparents were born in America. They descended from Scots-Irish and English settlers. They were farmers who worked hard and valued common sense. Many of them had lived in Kentucky, Virginia and the Carolinas until land became available in the new frontier of Missouri.

Both Harry and Eddie were men with strong convictions. Eddie had received instruction in the Jewish faith and, as an adult, embraced Reform Judaism, while Harry considered himself a Baptist. Even though they both lived in the Kansas City, area, Harry and Eddie were not friends until they joined the army.

Eddie and Harry lived and fought together as soldiers in the United States Army against the armies of the German Empire. The war brought out their talents. Harry achieved the rank of Lieutenant and then was promoted to the rank of Captain. He became the Commander of Battery D in the 35th division in France during World War I. His men looked up to him. He was not only their leader, but a successful leader. Remarkably, he managed to bring them all back to America safety.

**World War I Canteen**

Since Eddie had a gift for words and sales, Harry selected him to run the canteen. To set up the shop, the soldiers each gave two dollars to purchase supplies, candy, magazines, and toiletries. After six months, the money was refunded to the men as the unit's store became a thriving business. In fact, it was the only store in the whole army during World War I that made money. Harry would always admit that Eddie was the one who ran things, and that was why they made such a good profit. In fact, Harry would jokingly call Eddie a "crackerjack" because he was such a good businessman.

During the war with Germany, Harry and Eddie served with the U. S. army in France and fought outdoors in long ditches called "trenches," where many soldiers were killed in battle. It was a terrible war. Weapons such as automatic rifles, machine guns and poison gas injured more people in one year than in all four years of the Civil War in America. However, not one of the soldiers in Harry's unit died during the war.

**Soldiers in the trenches during World War I**

Life as a soldier was lonely. The men missed their families and especially the ladies they dated before the war. Harry wrote to his girlfriend, Bess Wallace, and Eddie wrote to his sweetheart, Bluma Rosenbaum, every day. When Eddie would ride into town to get more supplies for the unit's store, he would mail the letters and pick up their incoming mail at the post office.

The war was hard, but the soldiers continued to work together to do all they could to keep America free. Through the hardships of World War I, Eddie and Harry became the best of friends.

**Trinity Episcopal Church and B'nai Jehuda Reform Temple**

After America and its Allies won the war, Harry and Eddie went back to live in Missouri and married their childhood sweethearts. Before the war, they were young men. When they returned, they were experienced soldiers who had given years of their lives to serve America. Because of this, both men married much later than they had planned. Harry was thirty-five when he married Bess Wallace at the Trinity Episcopal Church in Independence, Missouri. Eddie was in his late twenties when he married Bluma Rosenbaum at B'nai Jehuda Reform Temple in Kansas City.

Bess and Bluma were beautiful girls, and their families soon expanded. Harry and Bess had one daughter they named Margaret. The children of Eddie and Bluma were named Elinor and Gloria. Both Harry and his daughter Margaret were musicians. One of Eddie's daughters, Gloria, took piano lessons, and when Harry visited Eddie's house, he found time to play a duet on the piano with Gloria.

Harry and Bess Truman

**Inside the Truman & Jacobson Haberdashery**
**~ Eddie on left and Harry on right behind counters**

Harry and Eddie enjoyed looking their best. Eddie had experience in merchandising. Beginning at age 14, he worked in a dry goods store. After the war Eddie and Harry opened a haberdashery—a men's clothing store—called "Truman and Jacobson Haberdashery" in Kansas City, Missouri. Harry called it "the shirt store." Eddie did the buying for the store and Harry was the bookkeeper. They took turns waiting on the customers. Many people bought clothing from them, including their army friends from the war. Others came to the store just to visit with Harry and Eddie. In fact, the haberdashery became the headquarters for both local and national news. Former soldiers would go there to find out what Harry and Eddie had heard from their army friends who also visited the shop.

Customers said the store was a "sharp place." The shop had a great layout and people could easily find the things they wanted. Just like in the war years, Eddie and Harry trusted each other. They did not need a contract or a signed agreement to operate their business together. They were true friends and did not take advantage of each other.

Sales were doing fine until 1921, when money began to lose its value. As the economy worsened, people could only afford to buy the basic things they needed to live. Eddie and Harry found themselves in financial trouble. They borrowed money to keep the merchandise in their store up to date. When some of their old friends fell on hard times,

Eddie and Harry loaned them money whenever they could. The economy became so bad that many independent businesses had to close, including the Truman and Jacobson Haberdashery. Their customers just could not buy new clothes, but had to make the old ones do. After the business failed, it took Harry and Eddie many years to pay off the store's debts.

**The Truman & Jacobson Haberdashery**

They both worked very hard at several jobs to pay off the debt from the Truman and Jacobson haberdashery business. At times, they had difficulty supporting their families. Eddie became a traveling salesman until later in life when he saved enough money to open his own store. Harry ran for the position of eastern judge of Jackson County, Missouri, and won the election. During his campaign, he stood for the improvement of roads and promised he would work to help Jackson County develop a better business management system. His campaign speeches presented some of the issues faced by the county and his ideas for possible solutions to the problems. Harry then ran for the office of presiding judge; again he won. Harry was known as a judge who was always honest and fair.

Statue of Andrew Jackson in Jackson County, Missouri

Jackson County was named after former President Andrew Jackson. He was a hero to Harry and his family not only because he, too, was of Scotch-Irish stock, but they also looked up to him as a man of courage. As a judge, Harry had a life-size statue of his hero, former President Andrew Jackson on a big horse, placed in front of the courthouse. He was given a little copy of the statue. He treasured the small statue and kept it in all the offices he occupied for the rest of his life.

During this time, the friendship between Harry and Eddie grew. Whenever they could, they played cards at Eddie's house or at Eddie's brother's house. (Eddie's brother was A.D. Jacobson.) They also went out to lunch together to eat ribs. Since Harry and his wife Bess lived in the house that belonged to his mother-in-law, Mrs. Wallace, Harry did not have many of his friends come to see him there.

After serving several terms as a judge, Harry told his wife Bess that he would like to run for Congress. This definitely was not what Bess wanted. She loved living in Independence, Missouri, in her mother's home, surrounded by their extended family. In addition, the Democrat Party leaders did not encourage Harry to run for Congress.

Around a year later, he was asked to run for the United States Senate by some of the same people who earlier had not wanted him to run for Congress. His wife Bess was supportive this time as she knew this was what Harry wanted. And he was elected! His talent for remembering everything, his problem-solving ability, and his work ethic enabled him to relate to the Missourians he would be representing.

Throughout Harry's time as a judge and a senator, Eddie tried to help him whenever he could. They met together and played cards periodically in the basement of Eddie's house with many of their old army buddies from Battery D in World War I. Even though they were still good friends, Eddie didn't ask Senator Truman for special favors.

In the meantime, a problem was developing in Europe. Eddie's people, the Jews, were suffering and needed help.

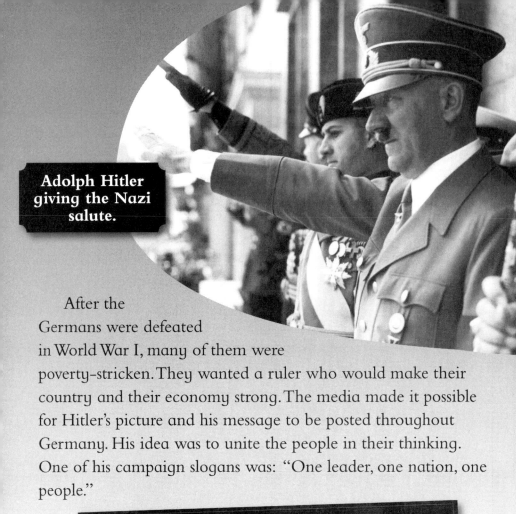

After the Germans were defeated in World War I, many of them were poverty-stricken. They wanted a ruler who would make their country and their economy strong. The media made it possible for Hitler's picture and his message to be posted throughout Germany. His idea was to unite the people in their thinking. One of his campaign slogans was: "One leader, one nation, one people."

## Ein Volk, ein Reich, ein Führer!

Adolph Hitler was a talented speaker, and when the German people heard him talk, they liked what they heard. He was a member of the Nazi party and ran for office on the platform promise that, if elected, the people would have good jobs and enough to eat. So persuasive were his speeches that some of the voters who listened to him thought Adolph Hitler would save their country from financial ruin. He was elected Reich Chancellor of Germany because people believed his promises that he would make Germany strong and prosperous again. Adolph Hitler called his government "The Third Reich."

Unfortunately, Adolph Hitler blamed Eddie's people, the Jews, for not only causing the loss of World War I but also for causing all of the country's other problems. He told this lie to the media. He shared it in his speeches and radio messages. Children in schools were encouraged to bully their Jewish classmates. Jewish Germans could no longer go to many public places such as restaurants, ballparks, movie theaters and swimming pools. Synagogues were burned, special taxes were placed on Jewish people and even sacred things like the Torah were destroyed.

Jews were sent to concentration camps aboard long trains.

Musicians wrote music and authors wrote books that made the Jewish people seem undesirable. All of this made their lives more and more difficult.

In the beginning Adolph Hitler did not tell the world about his plan to kill all the Jewish people living in Nazi Germany and its occupied countries. However, after he became Führer or Dictator of Germany, he ordered his soldiers to remove them, little by little, from their homes. Then people approved by the Nazi party took over their businesses. They were forced into ghettos (special enclosed villages). Some of the Jewish people were lied to and told if they would board trains, they would be taken to places where they could find work and have enough to eat. In truth, most of the people who got on the trains were taken to concentration camps where they were enslaved and starved. While many were selected for medical experimentation, others were killed in gas chambers.

"Who is to blame for the war?"

A gas chamber where thousands of Jews were murdered.

At the beginning of World War II, the newspapers and radios in the United States did not tell Harry, Eddie and people in America what Adolph Hitler and his Secret Police were doing to the Jewish people, the handicapped, as well as other special populations in Nazi Germany. Many people went into hiding all over Germany and in the countries the Nazi army had conquered. The Führer's government actually paid neighbors and people in their communities to inform them where Jewish citizens could be found. Once the Jews were betrayed, the Nazis took them away.

Some of the Jews were forced to dig their own graves, and some were shot by firing squads. Jewish people, handicapped children, and many adults were placed in the back of trucks and never seen again by their families. Others were gassed to death and then burned in huge ovens. Letters from people in Europe were sent to Jewish Americans as well as other citizens of the United States. The truth about what was happening in the Nazi Empire began to be known to Eddie and his family.

Liberators and underground networks in many nations saved some of the people deemed undesirable by the Nazis because they did not agree with the evil killing of innocent people. Using their minds, their hearts and their fortunes, these heroic people cared so much they endangered themselves and their families by rescuing men, women, and children from the death camps.

Meanwhile, the senator from the "Show-Me" state became known as the "The Man from Missouri." Now in Washington, DC, Harry Truman worked diligently on his committee assignments and for the good of the people. He exposed wasteful spending and was appointed to the Senate Special Committee to Investigate the National Defense Program that became known as the Truman Committee. Even the president of the United States, Franklin Roosevelt, took notice of the good things Harry was doing.

Eddie stayed in the Kansas City area and continued to work as a traveling salesman. If Harry needed him, Eddie would help or give him advice. Harry was a loyal friend to Eddie and abhorred the things that were happening to Eddie's people, the Jews. While Harry was a senator,

**Harry Truman working at his desk**

he spoke against Adolph Hitler's actions and wrote letters that enabled Jewish people to leave Nazi Germany and settle in Missouri. Those Harry was able to help needed to have someone, such as a family member or a relative, agree to sponsor them until they could support themselves in the United States.

Eddie and Harry had believed, along with many Americans, that they had been a part of winning the "war to end all wars." The truth was that the Great War, now known as World War I, did not end all wars. During the time Harry was a senator from Missouri, nation after nation, including the United States, entered World War II.

Franklin D. Roosevelt was effective as president and Commander-in-Chief of the United States military during World War II. Americans had confidence in him, and he communicated regularly by radio with them in his fireside chats. He comforted people throughout the war and is remembered for saying, "There is nothing to fear but fear itself." By the end of his third term of office,

**Franklin Roosevelt and Harry Truman**

President Franklin D. Roosevelt was in ill health. He needed to choose a running mate that would serve as vice-president for his fourth term of office. This person should be trustworthy, responsible, honest, and would labor with him not only to end World War II but also to work for the welfare of all people.

President Franklin D. Roosevelt chose Senator Harry S. Truman to run with him as Vice-President for his fourth and last term. On the evening when election returns were being counted, Major Joe Borenstine asked Elinor (Eddie's daughter) to marry him. It was clear the next morning that Roosevelt and Truman had won the election. Elinor could not find her dad and was told he had gone into Kansas City to see Vice-President-Elect Harry Truman. With her fiancé Joe, they drove into Kansas City to find Eddie and ask for his blessing. Eddie not only gave his approval, but brought Elinor and Joe to the victory party for the newly elected vice-president. Harry was playing the piano, but paused long enough for Eddie to share the good news about his daughter's engagement. Harry thought it was a good idea!

REGISTER AND VOTE

DEMOCRATIC

ROOSEVELT · TRUMAN

FOR LASTING PEACE·SECURITY FOR ALL

The Detroit Free Press EXTRA

## ROOSEVELT DIES OF STROKE; TRUMAN BECOMES PRESIDENT

Executive Stricken at Warm Springs

Eighty-two days after the election, President Franklin D. Roosevelt unexpectedly died. Newly inaugurated Vice-President Harry S. Truman was now the president of the United States of America! While Mr. Truman was well qualified to lead the nation, Mr. Roosevelt had not had time to fill Harry in on the details of all the governmental projects and decisions that he would face as president.

Because the president of the United States is also the Commander-in-Chief of the United States military, Harry worked with the military, the Congress, and with leaders of other nations to end World War II. President Harry S. Truman led America and her Allies to victory over Adolph Hitler's forces and the Axis nations that had aligned themselves with Germany.

Truman sworn in as President with his hands on the Bible.

25

American soldiers, as well as fighters from other nations, found concentration camps in the former Nazi Germany and occupied territories. To many American soldiers, this was the greatest atrocity they had ever seen. There were dead bodies that needed to be buried. People were sick and starving. Bugs were everywhere, and the stench of death and disease was almost unbearable.

**Prisoners from Ebensee concentration camp.**

Over six million Jews, and other people deemed undesirable by the Nazis had been murdered in World War II. It seemed that every family, had relatives who had perished during the war. The Jewish people who survived were freed from tyranny, but many who had lived through the Holocaust were sick, starving and traumatized and could not hold down a job. Most of them had no place to go. They were homeless because their belongings, their land, and their bank accounts had been stolen by the Nazis.

Release of inmates from a concentration camp.

Homeless survivors with no father or mother.

President Harry Truman was told of the many terrible things that had happened to the Jewish people during the war. He was saddened by what he heard, but his advisors in Washington, DC, warned him not to help them. The United States State Department, the United States Defense Department, as well as the British government, opposed American intervention in the Jewish problem in Europe.

In addition, some American Jewish leaders attempted to influence the president with money and promises of votes for his next election if he would help the Jews. But this did not work on Harry. He was thoroughly insulted that Americans would try to influence him in that way. In truth, Harry was not to be coerced by anyone about anything. He made the choice that he would let other people take care of the problems of the Jews in Europe.

Concentration camp survivors.

There were Jews who had been prisoners in the concentration camps during the Holocaust that survived. They were desperate for a place to call home. The majority of them were not welcome back to the countries where they lived before the war. After all, the Nazis and local Anti-Semites had stolen their homes, their goods, and their money. Some of the homeless Jewish people remembered that in the Bible it said they would one day return to the land of Israel.

Over a thousand years ago, the Ancient Kingdom of Israel had been conquered. Most of the ancient Jewish people had been forced from their homes and taken to other parts of the world while their homeland was ruled by other nations.

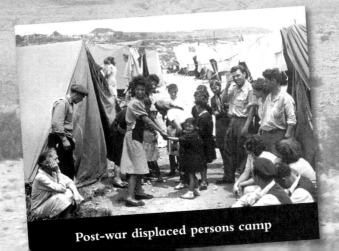

Post-war displaced persons camp

A famous Jewish biochemist named Dr. Chaim Weizmann was a hero to Eddie and many other people. Dr. Weizmann developed a process to make acetone, which was essential for the British war effort during World War I. Without supplies of acetone the British would not have been able to produce the ammunition needed for the battle against Germany. The British Prime Minister Lloyd-George and the Foreign Secretary Balfour were grateful for Dr. Weizmann's help and promised they would support efforts to create a homeland for the Jewish people in the ancient land of Israel.

**Balfour Declaration**

This promise, recorded in a letter from the British Foreign Secretary, Lord Balfour, to the Jewish leader, Lord Rothschild, was called the Balfour Declaration. This document was delivered to Chaim Weizmann, confirming British support from His Majesty's government for a Jewish "national home" in Palestine, which was previously the ancient land of Israel.

**Arthur Balfour**

Now after the terrible Holocaust, the survivors needed a place to live. Many of them wanted to go to the ancient land of Israel, even though it had become a desert. But the Jewish people were resourceful; they wanted to plant trees, farm the land, and build homes and cities where they could live safely.

Holocaust survivors bound for Israel!

A Shavuot service for survivors of Buchenwald concentration camp.

A new settlement in Israel

The treaties that ended World War I gave the British government a mandate or the authority to rule over the territory previously controlled by the Ottoman Turks. This included the ancient land of Israel. The British controlled immigration so the Jewish people were not allowed to move there without their approval. President Truman asked the British government to give the homeless Jewish people in Europe the opportunity to settle in the ancient land of their fathers. A joint Anglo-American Committee was formed to try to find ways to help the homeless Jewish population in Europe. In fact, some of the Jews who had been in concentration camps were still in holding camps supervised by the Allied Forces that included American and British soldiers. This Anglo-American Committee did not agree nor did they solve the problem. The issue of what to do with the homeless Jews in the former Third Reich was referred to the United Nations. For the new government of Israel to become a reality and allow the Jews to immigrate and rule their own land, Israel would have to be recognized by the United Nations.

Concentration camp survivors returning to the ancient land of Israel.

Back in Kansas City, Eddie wondered if Harry could help make it possible for the ancient land of Israel to become a nation. The Jewish people who survived the terrible Holocaust needed a place of their own.

Dr. Weizmann, the man who had been given the Balfour Declaration, knew something had to be done to help the Jewish people. Talks with the British were at a standstill. The American Jewish leaders had not been successful in convincing President Truman to intervene. So even though Dr. Weizmann was frail and in poor health, he traveled across the ocean to ask the president of the United States to support a new Jewish state.

President Truman refused to see him because of the disrespect and downright meanness of some of the American Jewish leaders. Harry had been slandered and threatened. A prominent rabbi actually told him that if he did not help with the homeless Jewish population in Europe, he would not win reelection.

Therefore, President Truman would not see Dr. Weizmann, nor did he want to hear what he came to tell him. Dr. Weizmann contacted Jewish leaders in American and told them that President Truman would not give him an appointment.

**Portrait of Dr. Chaim Weizmann**

American Jewish leaders and groups tried to talk to President Truman, but he would not discuss a Jewish State with them. In fact, Harry's appointment secretary was told that under no circumstances would the president see Dr. Weizmann or any representative of the Jewish Congress.

**President Harry S. Truman**

Finally, the international president of a notable Jewish organization involved in trying to help with the homeless Jews in Europe, remembered that Harry had a Jewish friend who was his former business partner. He called Eddie Jacobson on the phone and let him know that all efforts to see President Truman had failed and that Eddie was the "last hope" for a Jewish State.

Eddie did not want to go to Washington, DC, to ask his friend to help create a Jewish State because he knew there was little chance that Harry would change his mind. Even back when they were in the army, when Harry made up his mind, he never reversed his decision.

But Eddie knew this would make a difference in the lives of many hundreds of thousands of Jewish people who had suffered during the Holocaust, so he decided to try. He sent a telegram to Harry, asking him to meet with Dr. Weizmann. Harry refused. Eddie felt like "the hope" for creating the State of Israel depended on him. As a last resort, Eddie boarded a plane to Washington to talk with Harry personally.

**Harry's initial response to Eddie**

Because of their longtime friendship, Eddie felt that Harry would be glad to see him and catch up on old times. The two men were like brothers and had always been able to discuss any subject—personal as well as business matters. Unfortunately, Eddie did not have an appointment with the president and knew he needed a miracle to be successful. Furthermore, he knew Harry had left instructions that no petitioners on behalf of a Jewish homeland were to be permitted to talk with him.

Once in Washington, Eddie simply walked into Harry's office in the White House. No one stopped him. He walked past the security dogs, the Secret Service and Harry's secretaries, and entered the president's office, seating himself across from Harry's desk. Of course, Harry was happy to see his old friend and told Eddie it was amazing he had gotten in because he was not on his appointment calendar.

**Harry and Eddie**

Because Eddie had come in the interest of his people, he was willing to risk his friendship with Harry, and brought up the subject of a new Jewish homeland. Never in the decades spanning their friendship had Harry talked to him with such bitterness in his voice. He had been truly hurt by the way he had been treated by some of the American Jewish leaders. Furthermore, the president was convinced that the United Nations could deal with the problems of the homeless Jews in Europe. He had no intention of intervening. Eddie argued with the president in a way only friends can. He shared with Harry that Dr. Chaim Weizmann was in Washington and needed to meet with him to discuss the creation of a homeland for the Jewish people.

Because the situation had become so unpleasant with some of the Jewish leaders in America, Harry wanted nothing to do with the Jews' problems overseas. So he turned Eddie down, again refusing to see Dr. Weizmann. His mind was made up! He would not support a Jewish State so there was no need to listen to Eddie. The president wasn't alone; many leaders in America and around the world did not want the Jews to have a country.

Eddie thought about the disrespect some of the Jewish leaders in America had shown Harry. He shifted in his chair, scanning Harry's office. What could he do to convince his friend to help his people? Suddenly he had an idea when he saw the figurine that was always kept in Harry's office. He thought of Andrew Jackson as he looked at the little figurine of Andrew on his horse. Eddie also remembered the huge statue of President Jackson that Harry had erected in front of the Jackson County Courthouse in Missouri when he was a judge.

Harry S. Truman

Eddie knew that Harry's hero, the hero of his family, and the hero of many Missourians was former President Andrew Jackson. He remembered Harry reading books and pamphlets about Andrew Jackson back when they had the Truman and Jacobson Haberdashery in Kansas City.

Eddie turned to look his friend in the eye: "I have always known you have a hero. . . . Well, I have a hero, too—Dr. Weizmann, who I believe to be the most important Jewish person living today. I want you to know that he is a true statesman as well as a gentleman. He is old and sick, but he has traveled many miles across the ocean to this country to ask for a homeland for my people. Now, you won't see him just because some of the American Jewish leaders have insulted you? Dr. Weizmann has not insulted you. You are a fair person Harry Truman, and this just isn't like you. If you will see Dr. Weizmann, he will accurately inform you of the situation."

**Dr. Weizmann & Mr. Jacobson**

Harry tried not to listen. He drummed his fingers on his desk and then turned his back on his friend in his swivel chair. He looked out the window in silence for what seemed like centuries. Eddie knew Harry was thinking about changing his mind. He would not look at Eddie for a long time. Finally he swiveled around and faced Eddie. "You win, you bald-headed ★ ★ ★ I'll see him." President Truman then rang for his secretary, who scheduled the appointment with Dr. Weizmann.

Even though powerful forces opposed the United States' support of Israel, Harry kept his promise to Eddie. Dr. Weizmann met secretly with President Truman—entering through the East Gate of the White House so as not to be noticed by the press. Eddie could not go with him because his brother, A. D. Jacobson, was hospitalized, and Eddie needed to return to Kansas City.

East wing of the White House.

During their meeting, President Truman gave Dr. Weizmann his word that at the United Nation's vote, he would support and vote for Israel's statehood. The meeting that was scheduled for twenty-five minutes lasted forty-five minutes. Dr. Weizmann left, happy and grateful for the outcome.

President Truman & Dr. Weizmann

Immediately, there were problems. As soon as Eddie arrived back in Kansas City, he was told the president had changed his mind about helping the Jewish people. It had been announced by United States Representative Warren Austin at a United Nations Security Council meeting. Phone calls and wire communications came from all over the country to Eddie. Jewish people told him, "President Harry S. Truman is a terrible traitor." They accused him of breaking his promises and betraying the Jewish people. For days, Eddie was bombarded with complaints about his friend. People would not believe him when he told them they could have confidence that President Truman would keep his promise and do what he could to make it possible for the Jewish People to have a nation they could call home. Over and over again, Eddie defended Harry, telling callers, "Harry Truman is a man of his word. I'll believe what he said until the day he calls and tells me differently."

Several days later, Dr. Weizmann called Mr. Jacobson at his store, the Westport Men's Wear Company in Kansas City, Missouri. He said, "Just wanted to assure you that you can put your confidence in the word of President Harry S. Truman. May I remind you that your friend is the

Inside Jacobson's Westport Men's Wear store.

most powerful person in the world, so make sure the White House doors remain open. The lives of thousands of men, women, and children are depending on him."

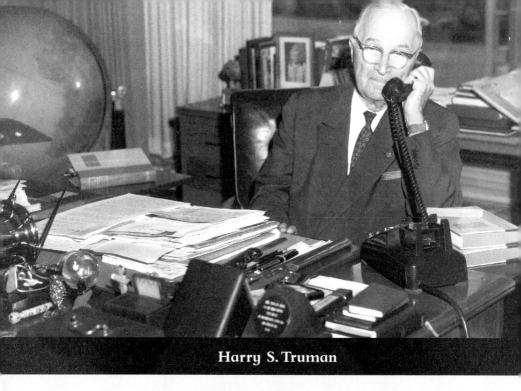

**Harry S. Truman**

Eddie's help was needed again, so he flew back to Washington. He met with Dr. Weizmann, who shared with him the importance of recognition by the United States of the new State of Israel. Like Dr. Weizmann, he entered the White House by the Eastern gate to avoid the attention of the media. Eddie quickly learned that of course, President Truman would keep his word to help the Jewish people establish a homeland in the ancient land of Israel. Harry reminded Eddie of the promises he had made to Dr. Weizmann. The rumors and accusations against President Truman were false, even though they had been published by the media.

Dr. Weitzman and President Truman knew the Jewish People would need more votes in the United Nations to become a country. Harry decided he would make calls to leaders of nations himself and ask them to cast their ballots for Israel. The phone calls were intense because every vote counted and a quorum or a majority of the countries in the United Nations were needed to support statehood for the Jewish people.

The United Nations resolution passed, and the nation became The State of Israel. A date was set for the British to end their authority over the land so the new country could be established. Dr. Chaim Weizmann was elected president of the newly formed State of Israel. He called Eddie Jacobson and asked him to be the temporary spokesman for the new nation. Eddie was willing to do whatever he could to help his people, the Jews, as long as his own country, the United States of America, was not harmed. Eddie was immediately given the task of bringing greetings to the president of the United States from the nation of Israel. He had been appointed by President Weizmann to be the unofficial envoy from the State of Israel to the United States. Now for the next four months, before Eddie entered Harry's office in the White House, the secretary would announce him as "The Ambassador from Israel."

United States document recognizing the State of Israel

Weeks later, President Truman put in a call to Israel's prime minister eleven minutes after Israel achieved sovereignty, thus making the United States of America the first country in the world to contact the new government of Israel and give her diplomatic recognition.

After waiting over a thousand years, the Jewish People finally were able to return to their ancient homeland, just as the Bible said they would. The people who had lost their land, their goods and their homes in the terrible Holocaust during World War II now had a place where they belonged. They were free to plant trees, farm the land and build homes and cities where they could create, govern, defend and live with their families.

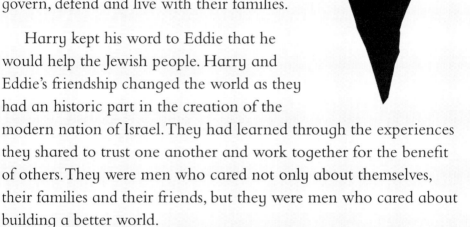

Israel

Harry kept his word to Eddie that he would help the Jewish people. Harry and Eddie's friendship changed the world as they had an historic part in the creation of the modern nation of Israel. They had learned through the experiences they shared to trust one another and work together for the benefit of others. They were men who cared not only about themselves, their families and their friends, but they were men who cared about building a better world.

Maybe someday you and one of your friends might do something to make the world a better place.

Tel Aviv, Israel

Mr. Jacobson died October 25, 1955.

Below are remarks by Harry Truman at one of the memorial services for his friend Eddie Jacobson.

"I don't think I have ever known a man I thought more of outside my own family than I did of Eddie Jacobson. He was an honorable man as I said in my memoirs, that I published not long ago. He was one of the finest men that ever walked this earth, and that's covering a lot of territory in my knowledge of people that I have seen, and I think I've come in contact with about as many people as any one man ever did. Eddie is one of those men you

**Harry speaking at a synagogue to honor his friend Eddie**

read about in the Torah, and I have a Torah that the president of Israel gave me that is one of the greatest things I own, and he issued an injunction as president of Israel, authorizing a Baptist to handle it. And I am of the opinion, that if you read the articles in Genesis concerning just two men—one of them was Enoch and the other, Noah—you'll find those descriptions will fit Eddie Jacobson to the dot. So when you honor Eddie Jacobson, you honor me, and I thank you for it. And I leave you with one thought, that the State of Israel will find stability and progress, and from Isaiah, 'They shall beat their swords into plowshares, and their spears into pruning hooks; nation shall not lift up sword against nation, neither shall they learn war anymore.' This is my prayer for peace. I thank you" (Krasnoff, 1997, p. 197).

## May 8, 1884

Harry S. Truman is born in Lamar, Missouri.

## June 17, 1891

Eddie Jacobson is born in New York City.

## 1917–19

Harry S. Truman and Eddie Jacobson serve in the 129th Field Artillery, 35th Division, U.S. Army.

## 1935–1945

Harry S. Truman represents the State of Missouri in the United States Senate.

## January 29, 1945– April 12, 1945

Harry S. Truman serves as Vice-President of the United States of America.

## 1945–1953

Upon the death of President Franklin D. Roosevelt, Harry S. Truman becomes president of the United States of America and is reelected for a second term of office.

## March 13, 1948

Eddie Jacobson walks into the president's office in the White House without an appointment to ask him to meet with Chaim Weizmann. Mr. Truman agrees to see Dr. Weizmann because of his friendship with Eddie.

## March 18, 1948

Chaim Weizmann goes through the East Gate of the White House and is escorted to meet with the President. During the meeting Harry Truman promises Dr. Weizmann that the United States will support the United Nations' recognition of the State of Israel.

## April 11, 1948

Eddie Jacobson goes into the White House through the East Gate unnoticed and meets with President Truman. Harry reaffirms the promise he made to Dr. Weizmann that he would recognize the new State of Israel.

| 1919-22 | 1922-24, 1926-34 | 1922-1945 |
|---|---|---|
| Harry S. Truman and Eddie Jacobson are partners in the Truman & Jacobson Haberdashery, Kansas City Missouri. | Harry S. Truman serves as a judge for the Jackson County Court in Missouri. | Eddie Jacobson is a traveling salesman in the clothing business. |

| 1945-1955 | February 21, 1948 | February 27, 1948 |
|---|---|---|
| Eddie Jacobson owns and operates Eddie Jacobson's Westport Menswear, Kansas City, Missouri. | Eddie Jacobson telegrams President Truman to request that he meet with Chaim Weizmann, president of the World Zionist Organization and the Jewish Agency for Palestine. | Harry Truman answers Eddie's telegram and refuses to meet with Chaim Weizmann. |

| May 14, 1948 | May 14, 1948 | May 17, 1948 |
|---|---|---|
| The British mandate expires, and a Jewish State of Israel is announced by the prime minister through the reading of a "Declaration of Independence at 6:00 p.m. EST." | President Truman calls David Ben-Gurion, Israel's new prime minister at 6:11 PM to give recognition by the United States of America of the provisional government of the State of Israel. | Chaim Weizmann is elected president of Israel's Provisional Council of State. Dr. Weizmann asks Eddie Jacobson to serve as his unofficial envoy to the White House. |

# Selected Resources

## Books

Devine, Michael J., ed. *Harry S. Truman, the State of Israel, and the Quest for Peace in the Middle East.* Kirksville, MO: Truman State University Press, 2009.

Devine, Michael J., Robert P. Watson, and Robert J. Wolz, eds. *Israel and the Legacy of Harry S. Truman.* Kirksville, MO: Truman State University Press, 2008.

Krasnoff, Sidney O. *Truman and Noyes: Story of a President's Alter Ego.* West Palm Beach, FL: Jonathan Stuart Press, 1997.

Radosh, Allis and Ronald Radosh. *A Safe Haven: Harry S. Truman and the Founding of Israel.* New York: HarperCollins Publishers, 2009.

_____. *Harry S. Truman and the Recognition of Israel.* Independence, MO: Harry S. Truman Library Institute for National and International Affairs to Commemorate the Fiftieth Anniversary of United States Recognition of Israel.

## Children's Books

Faber, Doris. *Harry Truman.* New York: Abelard-Shuman, 1973.

Leavell, Jr., J. Perry. *World Leaders Past and Present: Harry S. Truman.* New York: Chelsea House Publishers, 1988.

Shuter, Jane. *Prelude to the Holocaust.* Chicago, IL: Heinemann Library, 2003.

Stanley, George E. *Harry S. Truman Thirty-Third President of the United States.* New York: Aladdin Paperbacks, 2004.

Venezia, Mike. *Harry S. Truman: Thirty-Third President 1945-1953.* New York: Scholastic Inc., 2007.

## Papers

Harry S. Truman Papers, Harry S. Truman Library, Independence, Missouri

Eddie Jacobson Papers, Harry S. Truman Library, Independence, Missouri

Truman Library, Elinor Jacobson Borenstine Oral History

Truman Library, Gloria Jacobson Schusterman Oral History

Weizmann Archives, Harry S. Truman Library, Independence, Missouri

## Web Sources

A Few Humble Coins and the Making of Israel. Jewish Virtual Library: A division of American Israeli Cooperative Enterprise. Available: http://www.jewishvirtuallibrary.org/jsource/US-Israel/coins.html

Edward Jacobson Papers Dates: 1913-1974. Harry S. Truman Library and Museum. Independence, MO. Available:

http://www.trumanlibrary.org/hstpaper/jacobson.htm

## Correspondence

Notes from phone call 9-25-2010 and E-mail 9-27-2010 from Elinor Jacobson Borenstine, daughter of Eddie Jacobson.

# Photo Credits

Pages 12, 13, 14, 15, 20, 21, 26, 27, 29, 30, 31, 41, 42 Public Domain.

Pages 15, 16, 24, 40 Public Domain, Courtesy of Harry S. Truman Library.

Pages 17, 19, 33, 35, 36, 37, 39, 43 Copyright unknown, Courtesy of Harry S. Truman Library.

Pages 18, 23, 25 Public Domain, Courtesy of Missouri Digital Heritage Collection http://cdm16795.contentdm.oclc.org/cdm/landingpage/collection/trumanlib

Page 22 All Rights Reserved, Photo by Beverly Joan Boulware.

Page 27 Public Domain, Photo by Toni Frissell, 1945.

Page 28 Maabara, 1950 Courtesy of the Jewish Agency for Israel.

Page 28 CC BY-SA 2.0 Negev Desert, Israel http://flickr.com/photos/brewbooks/

Page 28 Public Domain, Buchenwald, Germany May 18, 1945. Courtesy of National Archives and Records Administration.

Page 30 CC BY-SA 2.0 On the ship to Israel. Courtesy Jewish Agency for Israel.

Page 30 Public Domain, Israeli settlement, Sokolov Street paving. Courtesy of the Jewish Agency for Israel.

Page 32 CC BY-SA 3.0 Chaim Weizmann, 26 March 1949. Photo by Mendelson Hugo. Source: https://commons.wikimedia.org/wiki/ File:Flickr_-_Government_Press_Office_%28GPO%29_-_President_Chaim_ Weizmann.jpg

Page 38 Public Domain, Photo by William Henry Jackson.